I0063051

Followership

B. Vincent

Published by RWG Publishing, 2021.

FOLLOWERSHIP

First edition. July 7, 2021.

Written by B. Vincent.

Also by B. Vincent

Bridge Pages
Business Acquisition
Business Bogging
Marketing Automation
Better Meetings
Conversion Optimization
Creative Solutions
Employee Recruitment
Startup Capital
Employee Incentives
Employee Mentoring
Followership

Table of Contents

Followership

L eonard Bernstein once said, the most difficult instrument to play in the orchestra is second fiddle, and Barbara Kellerman tells us. followership does not mean changing the rank of followers but changing their response to their rank their response to their superiors, and to the situation at hand. Anyone who studies leadership and management know that the best leaders know how and when to follow. Not only is followership a crucial characteristic for a person to have before they become a great leader, but it's also something that must be cultivated effectively among your subordinates in order for your leadership to be effective. So, the big question is, how, how do we properly embody this vital attribute on ourselves? And how can we encourage and cultivated among all of our team members in our workplace? In this course, we're going to teach you how to do exactly that. Studies indicate that around 80% of organizational success is a result of follower contributions. 86% of employees and executives said that a lack of collaboration or ineffective communication is a main reason of workplace failure. These statistics show that followership is an increasingly important area that businesses should focus on. Our course is going to consist of a series of critical discussion points.

These are designed to cover this broad topic as thoroughly as possible to encourage growth in these vital areas. And to facilitate a real and fruitful discussion within your organization about how you can eat improve on this essential characteristic, both at work and in your personal lives in general. Some of these will be pretty lengthy, and some will be relatively straightforward and brief. At the very end of this roadmap comes the most important final step. Discussion time do not skip this. This is the most important part of this training. When you finish this course, you need to spend at least an hour or so going over the questions we supply at the end as a group. Whoever's the head honcho in the group should designate a facilitator whose responsibility it is that each question is covered and that everyone time permitting is able to have their say, make sure all contributions are valued, all suggestions considered, and all opinions respected.

So, let's move into the first discussion point. Be content with your current job. As members of an organization, you recognize that that you all have different roles and responsibilities. A great follower understands that regardless of the differences, every role is important, and that working harmoniously is vital for the organization's growth. However, there can be times where you can grow envious of other members, especially if they receive more rewards and benefits than you. Another reason why you might envy other workmates is that maybe they're in a position that you so badly wanted for a long time. These are just some factors where we might feel that our current job or role is less important than others. To be a good follower. You need to practice humility and contentment. Recognize that an organization is like a body. Our body is composed of various organs, each having its own specific purpose. However, despite their different functions, every organ is important for the body to perform at its highest capacity.

The same is true for your organization. Though you may have a different role or an inferior position than others, you understand your worth and how your efforts contribute to the overall success of your organization. Having a content mindset not only avoids it well, but it also gives you a sense of self-respect. This in turn will boost your morale. Keeping you positive throughout each day. Do your best in your current role. connected with the previous point. comparing your position to others can lead you to feel that you should be doing your dream job instead of your present one. This may lead you to perform sluggishly at work, feeling that you should be doing more meaningful work than your current role. However, to be a great follower, you have to understand that in the end, it doesn't matter what you want. As an adherent of a company, you recognize that you were in a place where the organization needs you to be. So instead of weighing against another, appreciate your current assignment and make the most out of your situation. More importantly, prove your worth by demonstrating admirable qualities like proactivity, and leadership. As you maximize your current role, you will gain the respect of your associates and more importantly, your boss. In time you'll be seen as someone who is capable to take on more responsibilities. your patience and hard work will surely pay off once you've been rewarded with a more exalted role.

Even better. Imagine the feeling of finally achieving your dream job. For now, continue humbling yourself and do your best on whatever you're asked to do. understand things from a leader's point of view, do you often find yourself questioning your leaders' choices presuming that their decisions are always out of touch? Though it may not always be the case, we tend to feel this way because of a lack of perspective. A limited viewpoint may lead us to think that those in command are making mediocre decisions that are highly affecting the company. However, instead of being quick to judge, why not take time to understand things from their point of view, try to put yourself in their shoes and ask yourself if I were them. What should I do? You might be surprised at how much thought was put into every decision. When you see the world through their eyes, you'll start to understand the wisdom behind every decision.

This in turn helps you to put more respect in their positions. Moreover, understanding a leader's point of view motivates you to think alike, making decisions that are always for the greater good. Understand your organization's mission. With a lot of tasks on your plate, you may sometimes feel that your job is an endless loop of work that provides no sense of accomplishment. This lowers morale and decreases productivity. On the other hand, you and your team might be too focused on the other aspects of the business that you forget what you're actually trying to achieve the organization's mission. Great followers understand the company's mission, and they work with their heads up knowing that they're serving a larger purpose. Review your organization's mission, then take a look at your company's goals. Are they currently aligned with the mission? If so, then add improvements to reach the end goal faster, if not make the needed adjustments to keep the company back on track. Of course, this isn't a one-man job, you all need to work together to reach the mission. discuss it with your team. emphasize the importance of how each role helps the company to grow and evolve. Practice transparency in the workplace by having open communication. encourage everyone to share their ideas and suggestions on how to improve other aspects of the company. More importantly, hold your team accountable. set clear expectations from them when they understand how they share responsibility for the organization's future. This will motivate them to keep working at a high level. Show initiative. No matter what position we're currently in, we all can do more for our team.

A big problem though, is that we sometimes lack the initiative to do things. This may result from having a fear of criticism, self-doubt, and lack of faith in one's ability. However, a great follower understands that in order to get things done, somebody should make the first step. How can you show initiative in the workplace? Start small in your current work? Find ways to get work done more efficiently. practice speaking up starting from your next team meeting. Let people get used to hearing your ideas and suggestions. When you consistently offer valuable output, your voice will be heard over time. Once you start building your initiative muscles. You can then take it to the next level. Demonstrate decisiveness by being comfortable in making decisions. Think ahead by analyzing If current goals are aligned with the vision of the company, are you looking for more ways to show initiative in the workplace? Here are more practical suggestions. Seek more responsibilities, train or mentor others offer help to coworkers. volunteer to work with other teams and departments refer good potential employees, resolving interpersonal conflicts at work, anticipate problems and preventing it. Doing quality control for finished projects provide practical feedback. When people hear the word feedback, they often can note with fault finding nitpicking and complete disapproval. However, providing feedback is one of the most powerful tools you can use to motivate an individual to do even better. This is because feedback focuses on the action not the person. It's not a personal attack, but an honest and unbiased comment on their actions and behaviors. How can you properly provide feedback? Here are six practical steps. Number one, check your motives before giving out feedback. Remember that the purpose is to help improve a person's performance. You can only relay it by having a positive tone and by focusing on their strong points. Number two, ask for permission. This step often gets overlooked, but you'll be surprised at how much difference this can make.

A simple Hey, do you have a minute for a quick feedback can help them to mentally prepare regardless of if it's positive or negative. Number three, be timely. The sooner you give your feedback, the better. When you think about it. Feedback isn't about surprising someone, the sooner you do it, the more the person will be expecting it. Number four, Be specific. Avoid giving generalized comments for it can be confusing and might not be properly acknowledged. Instead, be frank, tell them straight on what he or she needs to improve. Number five, pause. After you've said your piece, pause, then ask the employee what he or she feels. give them time to process your feedback and hear what they have to say about it. Number six, suggest actionable steps ended with a positive note. Give them small actionable steps that they can take to fix a behavior or improve a certain skill. demonstrate a strong work ethic. What makes a good follower stand out is that they have a strong work ethic. work ethic is defined as having a combination of characteristics based on the principles of discipline and hard work. It is based on attitude and behavior. When a person has a strong work ethic, they understand the moral benefit and importance of work and how it contributes to your personal wellbeing a strong work ethic is important for achieving career goals.

When you possess a strong work ethic, you'll produce quality work, have a strong camaraderie with your team and be committed to taking your organization to new heights. When you prove yourself to be an exemplary worker more responsibilities and opportunities will come in your way. Do you want to improve your work ethic? Here are some practical suggestions. Get rid of distractions. Track your time, be organized. Practice time management. Maintain a work life balance. Have the courage to speak up. All companies encounter organizational problems. For instance, leaders may at times make poor decisions that have no clear direction and are not aligned with the organization's goals. You may have a strong headed or perverse coworker that highly affects the synergy of the team. At other times, your superiors can get really busy that they start to lack awareness for their team resulting to a lower workplace morale as a follower.

What are you going to do? Will you just sit there and let things be or are you going to do something about it? For you to exhibit followership, you need to have the courage to speak up regardless of how painful the truth may be for them to hear. A person displaying courage is not afraid to speak up and assert themselves when they feel strongly about a certain issue. This can be nerve wracking, especially if the one you're speaking to is your boss. Yet courage helps you to be bold and address the issue. More importantly, it helps you to offer advice and practical solutions. In addition to addressing an issue. Courage is also needed when you need to admit your mistakes. Nobody's perfect. So, there will be times where you will make careless decisions who will reasoning or bad judgment. However, it's easy for us to get puffed up with pride and let things pass. But when you have the conviction that you should make things right for the sake of the organization, it will strengthen your resolve to speak up, apologize and make the needed changes. Be collaborative. For a team to function well, collaboration is a must. A collaborative group is composed of people who constructively explore their ideas to make innovations and achieve a shared goal. A unique aspect of collaboration is that it's nonhierarchical. There is no seniority or rankings. Everybody is even handed and has an equal status. If you're a leader, how can you encourage a collaborative environment? Consider these suggestions. identify individual strengths, set realistic expectations, use collaboration tools, celebrate every win, encourage receptiveness develop a strong sense of community delegate tasks. When an organization is focused on collaboration, team members will feel that they are serving a higher purpose. It creates a loose and friendly environment that uplifts the overall vibe of the company. It enhances an individual's problem-solving skills and fosters responsiveness.

Having a collaborative environment makes all team members feel involved knowing that every contribution is highly appreciated. Display loyalty. Good followers understand that in order to be committed to the organization success, they have the obligation to be loyal. loyalty is such a valuable trait for it helps you to stay faithful even when various problems arise. However, as a follower, your loyalty should not be to those who are in command. Rather, your strong allegiance should be to the organization, not to a given leader at any given point in time. Here's how followers can display their loyalty at the workplace. Do your job well. Take pride in your work. continue to find ways to improve be a team player be determined. Put feedback into action. On the other hand, if you're the manager, how can you increase employee loyalty? Here are some ways cultivate their potential. Openly express how much they mean to the company. Avoid micromanaging defend them. Loyalty encourages your team to do their best in their work. Having loyal employees means that you have workers who perform productively and efficiently. This helps boost the company's performance resulting in more sales and increased profits. Additionally, staff loyalty lowers the rates of employee turnover. This means that as the organization progresses, your employees will be there for you in the long haul. possess good judgment. A good follower understands the consequences of their decisions.

So, they think first before taking action. Possessing good judgment is important for we make decisions every day. What are the components of good judgment? Consider these four ways. Listen attentively, team members must learn how to listen to each other. They should be able to gain insight from feeding off of each other's ideas. They should be open and honest with each other, and they welcome all perspectives. Seek diversity. For teams to exercise good judgment, all members shouldn't be caught in the same cloth. Instead, the team should be composed of individuals having diverse skills and experiences. This helps not only for gaining insight to other aspects of the business, but it's also a good way to hear opinions from different angles include different depths of experiences. In order to gain collective insight. It's important that members are composed of individuals having an assortment of experiences, the more experienced the group has, the better judgment will be at the same time. It should also include those who are inexperienced and those who have different experiences. factor the consequences before execution. Before even finalizing a decision, the team should carefully consider the factors that will take place once the decision has been executed, what changes will be significant? Who were those that will directly be impacted by it? If you are prepared for the potential results of a decision, you can be confident that you will perform a strong execution. good judgment is the key to unlocking your potential. When you practice good judgment, you will gain practical wisdom and moral reasoning. It's a sign of maturity and having this opens the door for more responsibilities and opportunities. Show honesty. We all know that honesty is the best policy, but do we really practice it? For others, they find honesty to be better in theory than in practice. They tend to avoid voicing opinions, frustrations, and disappointments.

Instead, they share it out through employees by forms of gossip, or just keeping it to themselves resulting in internal frustration. Having a tight and dishonest environment is not healthy for the organization. And this will eventually lead to conflicts. If you really want your business to evolve and grow. Transparency should be practiced. If you're the manager, give your employees the freedom to express what's on their mind, you may be surprised by what they have to say. Letting them voice out their thoughts may actually help you get a reality check. Although your employees can be brutally honest, they will no doubt help you to identify the company's flaws and make the needed changes to fix the problems. When you cultivate an honest environment in the workplace, people will become happier and more productive. More importantly, honesty builds trust and confidence to the organization. How can you foster honesty in the workplace? Here are five tips. Set aside judgment give everyone the freedom of expression, even to those who you personally don't agree with.

When you let your employees feel that their opinion is heard and valued, you will build strong relationships that are based on transparency. Get it off their chests, after every meeting have a short portion where members are given an opportunity to voice out their concerns, frustrations, or anything that they want to get off their chests. Having this practice at work actually strengthens the camaraderie knowing that you can freely express your thoughts among colleagues. Listen and implement. Practicing honesty in the workplace doesn't limit to simply giving people an outlet to express their emotions, you have to make sure that you actually do something about their concerns. If employees see that their thoughts and opinions matter, they will be empowered. This strengthens their loyalty to the company. Let them justify. If an employee wants to voice out an opinion, make sure that they can back it up with facts and evidence. More importantly, they should be prepared to provide solutions. After all, making change is what's most important. And now it's discussion time. The most important part of this training whoever's the head honcho in the group should designate a facilitator whose responsibility it is that each of the questions you see on the screen is covered and that everyone time permitting is able to have their say, make sure all contributions are valued. All suggestions considered and all opinions respected.

Don't miss out!

Visit the website below and you can sign up to receive emails whenever B. Vincent publishes a new book. There's no charge and no obligation.

https://books2read.com/r/B-A-QWUO-LIFQB

BOOKS 2 READ

Connecting independent readers to independent writers.

Also by B. Vincent

Bridge Pages
Business Acquisition
Business Bogging
Marketing Automation
Better Meetings
Conversion Optimization
Creative Solutions
Employee Recruitment
Startup Capital
Employee Incentives
Employee Mentoring
Followership

About the Publisher

Accepting manuscripts in the most categories. We love to help people get their words available to the world.

Revival Waves of Glory focus is to provide more options to be published. We do traditional paperbacks, hardcovers, audio books and ebooks all over the world. A traditional royalty-based publisher that offers self-publishing options, Revival Waves provides a very author friendly and transparent publishing process, with President Bill Vincent involved in the full process of your book. Send us your manuscript and we will contact you as soon as possible.

Contact: Bill Vincent at rwgpublishing@yahoo.com www.rwgpublishing.com

www.ingramcontent.com/pod-product-compliance
Lightning Source LLC
Chambersburg PA
CBHW030537210326
41597CB00014B/1190